D1370424

THE NEW CAMPUS IN BRITAIN:

Ideas of Consequence for the United States

by RICHARD P. DOBER

EDUCATIONAL FACILITIES LABORATORIES

Library of Congress Catalogue Card #65-23604

Additional copies are available from the offices of
Educational Facilities Laboratories
477 Madison Avenue
New York, New York 10022

CONTENTS

FOREWORD

Higher education in Great Britain differs from the United States in academic customs, number of institutions, and resources. Like the United States it faces a crisis: the number of prospective students is growing faster than the places available. To meet the demand, plans have been put forward to establish new universities, to raise the status of other schools to university level, and to expand existing institutions well beyond their present enrollments.

In anticipation that this ferment might yield ideas pertinent to the American scene, EFL asked Richard P. Dober, campus planner and author, to examine the current physical developments in Great Britain today. Mr. Dober, who was in England to address the special planning seminar convened by the Architectural Association and the Royal Institute of British Architects at the University of Sussex last summer, agreed to do so.

This report on the implications of the British campus development scene is the result. We feel these ideas from Great Britain are of significance for the United States.

EDUCATIONAL FACILITIES LABORATORIES

BRUNEL shopping arcade from the ri

Out of conflict and controversy Great Britain emerges as a design laboratory, yielding ideas of consequence for the American campus.

One gains perspective on Britain's contributions by understanding that the significant events are less than four years old. At the end of World War II most development in higher education was placed under control of the national government, and important measures were taken to improve the quality and availability of facilities. Colleges of Advanced Technology were started, with university equivalent degree programs. As the postwar children came of age, the scale of national grants for construction and operation was increased, and techniques for selecting students for entrance were improved. Expansion at Cambridge, Oxford, and in the Civic Universities was encouraged. Institutions such as Leicester and Hull advanced from collegiate to university status, and two new universities were started: Keele (1949) and Sussex (1961).

Because of natural increase in population and an ever increasing percentage of qualified students desiring higher education, these measures failed to keep pace with demand.

In typical British manner, the clamor for political remedy was met by the appointment of a committee, in this case the Special Committee on Higher Education (1961). Chaired by Lord Robbins and charged with the task of formulating a national policy, it spent two years visiting foreign countries and English counties searching for information, opinions, and data.

The Committee's summary report (1963) stunned the nation and won national approval. More copies of the report were purchased by the general public than any other document printed by Her Majesty's Stationers, before or since.

Robbins recommended that the number of places in higher education be increased from 216,000 in 1963 to 390,000 by 1973 and to 560,000 by 1980. The Committee outlined steps to reduce the relative importance of Cambridge and Oxford. Many existing universities, whose enrollments ranged from 2,000 to 5,000 students, were asked to plan for 8,000 to 10,000 places. Six new universities were started at once: East Anglia, York, Essex, Lancaster, Kent, and Warwick. By 1964 three already had students studying on campus; all will have permanent buildings opened by the end of 1965.

Against this background the American planner seeking ideas and innovation in design found British university development in the summer of 1964 as exciting as it was perplexing.

First off, some British educators suggested that Great Britain was falling behind other leading countries in the provision of places. Britain aims at 17 per cent of the age group eligible for enrolling for full-time higher education in 1980. The United States admitted 40 per cent in 1963.

During the pre-election fever basic issues were thus raised again: how many students should be accommodated? how many colleges and universities should be started? what kind of curriculum was necessary? what kinds of housing policies? what kind of sites, urban or rural?

In the center of the intellectual turmoil were the new university Vice-Chancellors. Postwar trained, forward-looking, strong-viewed, and strong-willed, each has been matched with skillful architects similarly firm in their own beliefs. All were politely contentious toward one another.

Finally compounding all the uncertainties were the ambiguous

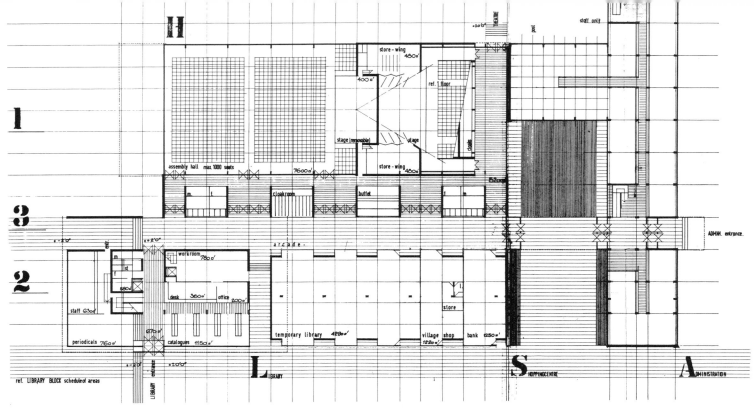

Brunel College of Advanced Technology. Ground Floor Plan: Library, Shopping Center, and Administrative Center. Architects: Richard Sheppard, Robson and Partners.

Battery Tractor used at Fallowfield -
University of Manchester.

Oxford University, Physics Building.
Architects: Ove Arup and Partners.

policies of the University Grants Committee, the fund-dispensing arm of the national treasury. UGC's decisions to date seem to be molded more by diplomacy than basic research. It regulates the speed, quality, and quantity of university construction but without any apparently firm and comprehensive policy.

It is a bureaucracy that does things nicely. A newly appointed Vice-Chancellor, expecting all kinds of red tape and regulations, was pleasantly surprised to receive as his mandate from UGC a simple letter welcoming him to the position and authorizing him to proceed with the planning.

A good example of UGC's technique is the way it handles funds for new construction. UGC has, in theory, devised a formula that protects the inept and rewards the clever. For each facility type a minimum square footage standard per user is established, and at the same time a maximum cost allowance is set which no one may exceed.

Despite all the indecision and travail, the ferment is a productive one, as the emerging designs indicate. While searching for solutions Britain has shopped well. Transatlantic and continental influences show through, especially in housing patterns, urban campuses, and co-ordinated systems of industrialized construction.

Adaptation rather than imitation, however, is the guiding principle. Even in details some old ideas, largely untested elsewhere, are now usefully at work; for example, the slow-moving service cart which keeps pedestrian-scaled sectors of the campus free of service trucks and automobiles. But in such critical areas as instructional "hardware"—gadgets and gimmickry—things have not advanced beyond the most elementary audio-visual aids.

The most striking synthesis is the continuous teaching environment, a physical form that preserves communication and contact between all parts of the institution while allowing external accretion and internal change. The many ways in which this is being done are detailed later in the report.

Within this growth context British attempts to reduce anonymity in the large institution have immediate application to a topical American dilemma. Too often the rigid distinctions between instructional, communal, and residential buildings reduce the opportunity for casual and undirected attachment to a fixed point in space. A sense of belonging is lost, and easy communication between members of the institution may be blurred.

The resulting problems may be overcome by a physical design that spreads activity points—meeting places, so to speak—throughout the campus rather than concentrating them in one place.

For the Lancaster long-range plan (see page 56), the architects have placed all communal facilities on the ground floor and then stretched them along a "street" that runs the length of the campus. Variations in this design theme are also shown later in plans for Essex, Surrey, and Warwick.

This attitude towards communality appears even in schemes where it is not possible to disperse activities. Richard Sheppard breaks down the old stereotype categories of building-by-function in his work at Brunel College of Advanced Technology. Bank, library, assembly hall, buffet, book store, and administrative offices are combined into a central facility. Later, through a decanting process, the library and administrative offices will expand laterally into their own separate but connected buildings.

1.

3. Nuffield College, Oxford.
Harrison, Barnes and
Hubbard, Architects.

3.

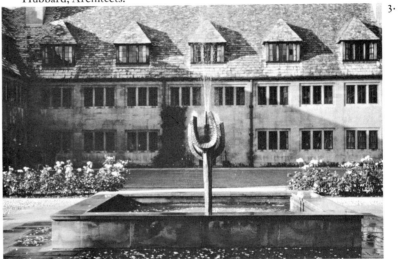

1, 2. Harvey Court, Cambridge.
Architects: Sir Leslie
Martin and Colin St. John.

2.

4.

4. Peterhouse, Cambridge.
Architects: Sir Leslie
Martin and Colin St. John.

HOUSING PATTERNS

The idea of encouraging a sense of belonging to the larger institution, while at the same time securing attachment to a smaller and more comprehensible segment, is further advanced in the design of new housing patterns.

While residential accommodations are considered a central feature of English collegiate life, only 25 per cent of the students are housed "on campus," a figure that has not varied much since 1930. The remainder reside at home or in lodgings. Because of the general housing shortage and the fact that most of the new universities are being developed outside suburban areas, significant changes in the quantity and character of housing are under way.

Four different patterns can be observed: the Oxbridge, the York, and the Essex prototypes, and the urban hostel.

Changes in the Oxbridge models are more of form than function. Good examples of the recent transition in architecture are Nuffield College, Harvey Court, and St. Catherine's. They continue the older quadrangular way of life, essentially being a series of linked study-bedroom accommodations with library, dining hall, porter's lodge, and Master's accommodations attached. Like Peterhouse, the first college building with a lift in Cambridge, they are expensive, imaginatively designed, beautifully constructed, and outside the mainstream of what is intended for the new universities.

The urban hostel, or residential hall, can be traced back to the nineteenth century as an attempt to give those living outside the residential college something more than a place to eat and sleep. It has become a major educational force, providing the student with social experiences and contacts not entirely divorced from his intellectual life.

Anticipating an expansion in enrollments and a parallel growth in housing, UGC surveyed housing at home and abroad (1962) in order to establish reasonable standards for funding this type of construction.

The UGC committee declared that the basic social unit in the new housing pattern should be a friendship group of 12 to 14 students, each having his own study-bedroom, and each sharing a "working" social center that takes the form of a small kitchen for breakfast and snacks and a common room.

These basic units would be combined into halls of up to 500 students each. Each hall in turn would support a dining room and special interest rooms for activities requiring the support of larger numbers than the basic social unit, such as theater, hobby, sports, and political organizations.

While designing the Princess Gardens Hostels for Imperial College London, Richard Sheppard and Partners further investigated the pros and cons of these arrangements, which are fundamentally Scandinavian in origin.

Sheppard's work intimates that the double student bedroom in the United States may be an anachronism, perhaps unduly prolonging the weaning period from home to collegiate life. Sheppard also believes that the single dormitory room is "unlikely to be really humanely satisfactory if it's less than 120 square feet. The furniture should be movable, not fixed, to allow the student to organize his own environment."

The Imperial College Halls are also significant because they are the first high-density residential schemes in England, about 1,500 single study-bedrooms in three major buildings.

The College wanted each 150 students gathered into halls of residence, each with a distinct identity. To retain a sense of enclosure for the park and to continue the terrace effects which are typical of the neighborhood, the halls are planned as horizontal layers, with one set of communal facilities placed under three floors of study-bedrooms. Stairs are placed along the communal floor, each serving 24 student bedrooms, 8 to a floor. Each 8-room set has its own service rooms. The stairs are linked to social and recreation rooms along the communal floor, which in turn serves as an entry to the halls above.

Changes in site levels have enabled the architects to fit university-wide common rooms for student and academic staff on the south side of the complex along a major pedestrian path that leads to the teaching buildings at the west. Thus the hall becomes a central place for the entire institution.

A second recent high-density scheme, Fallowfield—University of Manchester, responds to housing problems particularly associated with the Civic universities, many of which are located in central urban areas with limited possibilities for expansion on adjacent land. In these instances instructional areas, housing, and sports facilities are frequently forced onto separate sites.

Fallowfield is just a mile and a half from the academic core and fortunately adjacent to the University's playing fields. Conceived as a self-sufficient satellite campus for housing, it will eventually provide quarters for 3,000 students and staff in three multistory study towers, several 3-story courtyard accommodations, and 3- to 5-story terrace buildings.

Single and married students, graduates and undergraduates, tutors and wardens can be fitted into the several housing types. In line with the UGC recommendations the residents are grouped, with accompanying communal facilities, into social and friendship patterns appropriate to their age, sex, marital, and educational status.

The 14-acre site includes an administrative building, library, and assembly hall. The latter can seat 400 people and contains smaller function rooms and bar. It will be used for dances, lectures, and formal and informal meetings. During school vacation the hall can be used for nonuniversity conventions and the nearby residences will provide hotel space.

Dining facilities are unique because the physical arrangements create competition among the chefs, and the quality of food has risen accordingly. Food storage and preparation are handled in a central building. The materials are then carted to dispersed kitchens and dining halls where they are cooked and served. Students are permitted to eat where they choose, and naturally favor the hall with the best food. No need to wait for monthly waste reports to spot monotonous diets and poorly cooked meals!

Because they start on fresh sites, the new universities have the opportunity to originate housing patterns uniquely their own. York and Essex illustrate two different philosophies and design forms.

The plan for York is based on an expanding series of "colleges" to which each student and a proportion of the staff are attached for their whole time in the university irrespective of whether they are in residence or not.

Each "college" of 300 students (150 of whom live in) provides the major focus of social activity for the attached staff and students, and contains teaching as well as residential and communal accom-

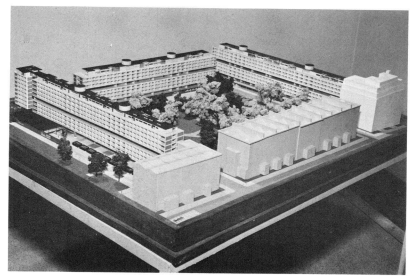

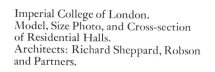

Imperial College of London.
Model, Size Photo, and Cross-section
of Residential Halls.
Architects: Richard Sheppard, Robson
and Partners.

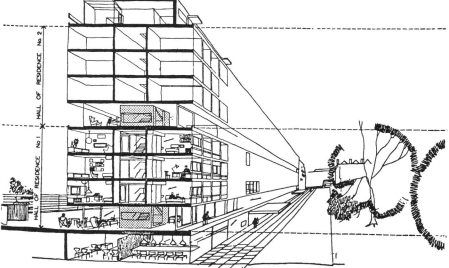

Tower Block at Fallowfield College,
University of Manchester.
Far Right: Size Plan.
Architect: Building Design Partnership.

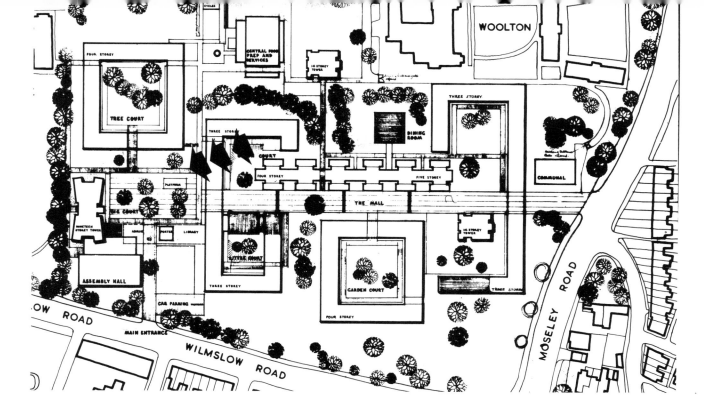

modations of various kinds.

The York scheme is further described on pages 48-53. The major criticism levelled against the York archetype is that it may be a nostalgic reflection of the Oxbridge ideal and thus out of context with the twentieth century.

York's spokesmen reply that there is need for giving young people a center of loyalty, smaller than the larger unit of the whole university, and for bringing about some measure of integration in their living, learning, and social activities.

The university planners at Essex decided that self-contained flats would provide the most suitable accommodation in these days of growing independence and self-sufficiency among the young people —at least they wanted to encourage the idea.

Housing at Essex will take the form of 14-story tower buildings, sited within five minutes' walk of the academic center. (See illustrations pages 42-44.)

The towers will contain study rooms for those living off-campus and bedroom-sitting rooms for those in residence. Both groups of students, say 7 and 20 of each, will share certain common rooms and kitchens. Men and women will live in the towers, usually on separate floors. The top story will serve as flats for unmarried staff members, the one below for married research and graduate students.

The Vice-Chancellor, Dr. A. E. Sloman, summarized the purpose: "The University is a community where the student is guided in the first stage of a lifelong task of self-education, a community whose concern is not just with the pursuit of learning but with the fulfillment of lives."

For the American scene is it York versus Essex? Not necessarily. The conscious formulation of connections between educational philosophy and housing goals is the idea of consequence.

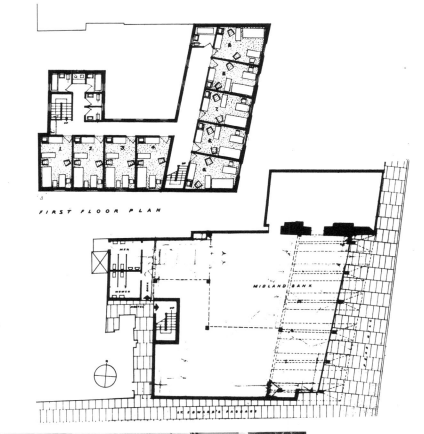

FIRST FLOOR PLAN

Market Hostel, Cambridge.
Architects: Architect's Co-Partnership.
Interior view of typical room.
Ground floor and first floor plan.
South facade and approach along St. Edward's Passage.
Next page: Street view of Market Hostel.

York and Essex—like their new university counterparts, Sussex, Norwich, and Lancaster—have started on generous estates and farm lands outside the core cities of their respective counties. As a result, a self-sufficient urban environment has to be created on predominantly rural land with a minimum of funds. Ingenuity has been taxed, but not to disfavor.

The dilemma of putting urban institutions on rural sites is due in part to the fact that Great Britain has developed at a density 10 times greater than the United States. Coupled with a staggering economy, this makes it difficult to start universities afresh on occupied sites without extensive dislocation and heavy investments.

To some English educators and their architects, the ideal university form *would be* an urban infilling, that is, an entire sector of the city where university buildings would be scattered about in a pattern similar to the University of Paris.

Oxford and Cambridge, of course, have grown this way over the centuries, more by accident than design, but the results are particularly attractive.

On a deliberate basis this approach holds great promise for a country which must extensively renew and redevelop its central city areas. Advocates of the scheme realize that it is not yet possible under the present crash programs, which cannot be postponed while waiting for land assemblage.

Two examples of intelligent exploitation of the urban environment already have been constructed: the University of Strathclyde in Glasgow and the Market Hostel in Cambridge. They point the way to opportunities which might easily be grasped in similar circumstances in the United States.

In Cambridge the Market Hostel combines study-bedrooms, for 21 undergraduates, with a bank. The residential units are grouped around an L-shaped airwell above the first floor. The site is "central to everything."

Strathclyde is a College of Science and Technology in Glasgow, just gaining university status under the Robbins recommendations. Through 1960 the school, without success, had requested the Glasgow City Corporation for a share of an adjoining site scheduled for redevelopment under the Town Planning Acts. The City's re-use plan called for commercial development of this valuable frontage near the city center.

Like American cities the Corporation was reluctant to part with valuable land for institutional expansion at the possible loss of tax-producing ventures.

Further representation was made through the summer of 1961,

University of Strathclyde,
Glasgow, Scotland. Arts, Social Sciences,
and Library building.
Architects: Covell, Matthews
and Partners.
West facade of University building
above shops and parking decks.
Central reading room. Portal frames
carry structure and allow large spans.

and terms were reached whereby the University would be allowed to participate on the condition that its accommodations would not exceed one-third of the total redevelopment, that its capital investment would not exceed $2.1 million, that it pay a fixed percentage of the site rent when the site rent was agreed upon by the City and the developer, and that it would under all reasonable circumstances reach accord on matters of design and construction as quickly as possible when the developer was selected.

Desperate for expansion room, the University agreed to the terms and prepared a description of its requirements for the prospectus the City distributed among 30 interested parties. The Corporation's final program called for a mixed development of shops, car parking, filling station, offices, restaurant, and 80,000 square feet for the University.

With the steep site falling away from north to south it was decided to house all the requirements in three elements: an office tower and a university building over a podium block. The former could be reached at ground level on one street side and would be three stories above on the other.

The podium block was designed for full coverage with shopping at ground level facing the City's main shopping precinct. Two decks of parking were placed above.

A 13-story office block with 125,000 square feet of rentable office space faces a public concourse (including the filling station) and a public garden.

The Faculty and Library building is situated at the west end of the podium with the podium deck level providing 100 parking spaces exclusively for University use.

As the library will have the heaviest circulation, it is placed on the two lower floors of the University block, with the Arts and Social Studies Faculty on the two upper levels. Both are approached from a common entrance hall.

Library floors are arranged around a central reading room, with adjacent bookstacks placed at intermediate levels. Accommodations have been made for 600 readers, 250,000 volumes, office and service spaces.

The third floor contains the lecture theaters, staff and student common rooms, and the main administrative office. These are arranged in three wings which frame a roof garden.

The largest lecture theater has seats for 220, and there are two additional lecture halls for 80 students each. These are allowed "to wander in and out of the structural grid spaces to emphasize the informal planning." The top floor contains staff, tutorial, and seminar rooms.

The Strathclyde project gives strong direction to an unusual American opportunity: the university in the sky. As an earlier publication from EFL's Western Regional Center* has pointed out, air rights can furnish new building areas where additional land is not available. Central urban sites of this kind, when well located, can help stabilize core city development. Through imaginative urban development policies many users can share a single location in constructive collaboration.

To be successful such schemes will have to be conceived under less duress than Strathclyde and designed and constructed in less haste. Not that the concept of Strathclyde has failed—the Harvard-trained planner for the scheme, Brian Falk, anticipated future University use of the office block in his design, and the building now is being transformed into a University facility less than two years after opening.

*Community Colleges in Urban Settings, 1964, Stanford University, Palo Alto, Calif.

Perspective view, Domus System.

CONSTRUCTION

The restrictive economy measures that Britain faced after the war stimulated the application of prefabrication technology to the building process. Low cost, reduction of on-site labor, speed of erection, and the conversion of factories from war to peace were the chief objectives.

Through CLASP (Consortium of Local Authorities Special Programme) a co-operative effort by several county administrations pooled research and building techniques on a major scale, effecting economy, efficiency, and control over the construction of a common, flexible, prefabricated system. A 7-County Authority consortium (1958/9) carried out an $8 million construction schedule which became known as the CLASP system.

The basic elements are the 5″ non-continuous site slab foundation, light steel frame, timber roof and floors, gypsum partitions, timber joinery, and a variety of dry external claddings, all of which make for rapid dry assembly and many design options within the 40″ horizontal and 24″ vertical module, up to three stories high.

The success of the system rests on absolute cost prediction by large scale orders to component manufacturers through co-ordinated programing; efficiency of prefabrication and design detailing; and precision and standardization of construction and dry assembly methods.

York University is the first of the new higher educational institutions turning to CLASP. In this instance an advanced system— Mark IV—will be used in all buildings except certain laboratories where rigid, antivibration construction is necessary.

Considering the national building program, including university expansion, unusual demands will continue to be placed on the British construction industry. The size of the working force is not likely to increase, and the output per man, rather than modest savings in cost, is likely to become the critical factor. Accordingly, new building systems are being called for which will reduce the amount of site work.

Generally these systems continue dry construction techniques, with maximum use of factory-produced components. Modular planning will be widespread. Most of the new universities intend to use this rationalized form of building, which is also called the industrialized building process.

Studies to date indicate however that economy in use cannot be secured without continuity of contracts because of the site preparation, setting up, and pre-forming time involved. It is possible then that universities will engage contractors on a continuing basis, the idea of "contractor to the university" is not far off.

Investigations of various types of construction have been under way in the last three years. There is general agreement that for reasons of flexibility in height, form, and loading, and to secure insulation against noise, temperature, and fire, concrete as a structural material has substantial advantages. In precast form it also serves as a cladding material.

There are exciting signs that great steps forward in both design and technology will come about as concrete and the industrialized building process are used in building the new universities.

In the Social Sciences Building at Birmingham, entire wall sections with window framing have been cast in a single piece and then bolted to the concrete grid. Casting techniques and finishes are rapidly improving, as shown in a sampling of recent projects.

Handling of very large precast concrete units has been limited to date by the size of cranes available. At Sussex the architects were permitted to import French models. The work there would not have been possible otherwise. Under new licensing procedures larger cranes are now being manufactured in Scotland.

The experimental Domus system, designed by the architect Ronald H. Sims for Howard Farrow Ltd., suggests some of the possibilities. Super-sized wall panels, loadbearing internal walls, and slab floors are poured and assembled on the site. By mixing the basic units in various building heights and widths, and with sensitive siting and landscape, architectural variety can be obtained within a standardized construction system.

The Domus concept has been designed for residential accommodations but as a principle could be applied to other types of university buildings.

British designers are eagerly searching for other techniques which will allow a minimum number of elements to be combined into a maximum range of building types. Sophisticated solutions are not yet evident, but the search has moved from premise to promise and will be well worth watching as the new universities come into being.*

*For a report on the first U.S. school building system see: *SCSD: An Interim Report*, Educational Facilities Laboratories, 1965. For further information on British school building systems see *British Prefabricated School Construction*, Report Number 2, School Planning Laboratory, *Stanford University*, Palo Alto, Calif.

University of Birmingham, Detail, Social Science Building.
Architects: Howell, Killick and Partridge.

2.

3.

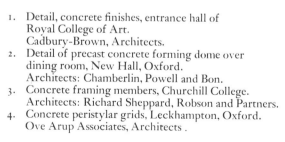

1.

4.

1. Detail, concrete finishes, entrance hall of
   Royal College of Art.
   Cadbury-Brown, Architects.
2. Detail of precast concrete forming dome over
   dining room, New Hall, Oxford.
   Architects: Chamberlin, Powell and Bon.
3. Concrete framing members, Churchill College.
   Architects: Richard Sheppard, Robson and Partners.
4. Concrete peristylar grids, Leckhampton, Oxford.
   Ove Arup Associates, Architects.

Brasenose College, Oxford.
Powell and Moya, Architects.

Detail, parking lot, University of Birmingham.
Casson and Conder, Architects.

1. Paving detail, Oxford.
2. Roof detail and planting tubs. Engineering Building, Imperial College, London.

AMENITY

Townscape and landscape are British traditions which have not succumbed to pressures of cost and timing. Amenity is present in recent design as it has been in the past. In the older university communities, skillful in-filling—a genuine regard for scale, materials, and site planning—has been carried out in situations that test ingenuity and sensitivity.

A superb example of fitting contemporary expression into a traditional setting are the extensions to Brasenose College, Oxford. It answers those who maintain that copying is the only answer, and equally refutes those who would prefer to ignore in their art that which already exists.

The Brasenose project contains study-bedrooms for 32 students in an irregularly shaped, four-story penthouse and courtyard building. Existing walls and gardens were incorporated in the scheme and in fact are used structurally. External cladding materials are limited to concrete and Portland stone, which in time will weather into colours like those surrounding. As leading critics have said—on a very difficult site, where they should never have been allowed to build anyway—the architects have produced one of the loveliest small buildings in England.

Handling the motor vehicle equally strains the designers' skills. The influence of the Buchanan report *(Traffic in Towns)* and the British new town experiences at Hull and Cumbernauld have affected the solutions to the extent that large, vehicular-free sectors are established in the campus plans, and motor traffic is segregated from pedestrians by means of tunnels and covered decks.

On open sites, such as Birmingham, well-designed masonry walls and birns screen the parking lots. Earth sculpture and landscaping are used to embellish the areas.

At all universities the surfaces of outdoor areas are treated with greater care than at American institutions. Paving materials, for example, are designed, not left to the whim of a hurried contractor.

Engineering Building,
University of Leicester.
Sterling and Gowan, Architects.

26

TEACHING BUILDINGS

To the transatlantic visitor British teaching buildings seem to be in the same stage as their American cousins: the best are now just under construction, but there are even better ones still on the drawing boards.

For typical reasons splendid opportunities were lost in the past 10 years: cramped sites ("We get a tall thin tower impossible to expand horizontally or something like a battleship lying across our front park"), occasionally inadequate briefs ("Don't do any detailed schemes, just show us how it will look"), a lack of long-range context into which to place the building ("We've been here for 40 years without a plan, it's disturbing to have to do one now"), and above all portrait architecture.

The latter is not peculiarly British, being part of an international tradition of designing for an individual, rather than a group client. Blocking the brain drain to the States by commissioning a new building for a promising professor has become a favorite ploy of university administrators. As a result, a scattering of architectural gems can be found, especially cut to the wants of the prominent staff member, but not very useful for those that follow. Low utilization is inevitable.

A cross-section view of the more typical education buildings, however, plainly shows the coercion of cost consciousness. Buildings now five or more years old were experiments in the systemitized construction process. Each architect made his own contribution to a variety of cladding, mullion, and closing materials while more or less following a modular structural design.

Not all the materials have held up to weather and use. With a repeating grid constantly pressed onto too many similar facades, monotony abounds.

Surface aesthetics were not improved with the introduction of the early type precast concrete elements. The "French finish" took hold: a general decrepitude in detailing that goes by the name "brut."

Exterior appearances aside, the majority of teaching buildings work well because of painstaking care in interpreting, clarifying, and responding to the academic program of the client. But therein lies the rub for the future. The crisis of numbers is only now pointing towards new directions in educational methods, and the older maps for the journey to excellence can no longer be slavishly followed.

In professional journals and in design meetings, the British architects have voiced concern about the present teaching technology and the probity of the ill-founded brief. In this light the Robbins universities should afford refreshing experiences for academicians and designers. The new universities have gained both inventive architects and Vice-Chancellors, all equal to the task of sharing the two sides of the creative endeavors necessary to developing new institutions. The balance remains to be struck, however, and the useful gains in both aesthetics and academic organization illustrated later in this report still need to be proven out.

The matrix for decision-making is following along these lines: quality versus quantity; initial construction costs versus continuing maintenance cost; tall and compact buildings for economy in land use and ease in communication versus an open site plan for easy expansion and infilling with the unknown; fixity of use versus flexibility.

On the "omniflexibility myth," architects such as Grenfell Baines have suggested that building for all-out flexibility is expensive, and overspending on it means inferior quality in vital places. Elaborate and expensive provisions for removable walls, ceilings, and even floors may be wasteful.

Baines believes that "people are easier to move than partitions." The costs of making a shell habitable are comparable in most buildings, the important differentials lie in equipment and services (utilities). In making flexible arrangements in these areas the designer has to operate on more than intuition, and perhaps this is why significant breakthroughs are yet to come.

"Paradoxically," comments Hugh Morris, designer for the University of Bath, "the program for a science building is usually more precisely detailed than that for an arts building; yet the best way to satisfy the brief is to design a building which is imprecise and loosely related to immediate needs. And in a similar vein a plan for a university centered around science may be abstractly construed the same way."

In his firm's work at Bath, the institution's growth will take a linear form, the central area is long, not round—"like the core in an apple, not the stone in a plum."

Growth takes place in two ways: by expansion at right angles to the central core, and by extension of the core itself, thus creating further potential growth. The major central activity areas would be established along the spine, as shown in the diagram and in the draft development plan to the right. Translated into physical form, the core would be a covered deck spine with all utilities and servicing from underneath. Teaching areas would extend outwards from the core, residential groupings filling in at selected points in the site development.

The basic diagram is one which appears in part in earlier schemes for other new British universities, and also can be traced to the experimental English new towns at Hook and Cumbernauld.

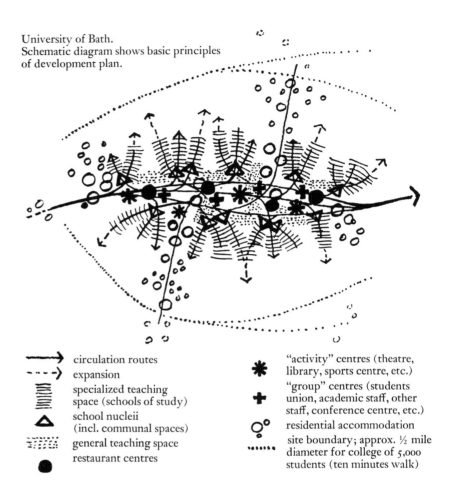

University of Bath.
Schematic diagram shows basic principles of development plan.

→ circulation routes
--→ expansion
≡ specialized teaching space (schools of study)
△ school nucleii (incl. communal spaces)
≋ general teaching space
● restaurant centres

✳ "activity" centres (theatre, library, sports centre, etc.)
✛ "group" centres (students union, academic staff, other staff, conference centre, etc.)
°○° residential accommodation
⋯⋯ site boundary; approx. ½ mile diameter for college of 5,000 students (ten minutes walk)

Right:. Development plan for long-range construction establishes major lines of movement, use zones, building locations, without commitment to a specific architectural solution.
Architects: Robert Matthew, Johnson-Marshall and Partners.

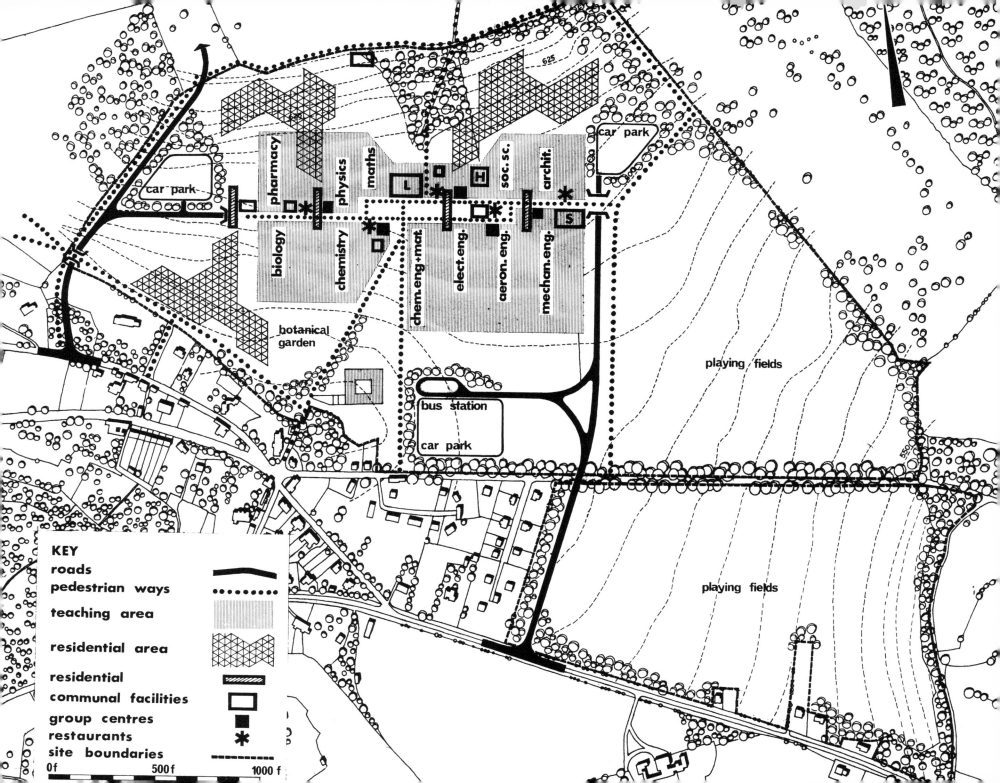

car park

car park

pharmacy

physics

maths

soc. sc.

archit.

L

H

S

biology

chemistry

chem. eng. + mat.

elect. eng.

aeron. eng.

mechan. eng.

botanical
garden

playing fields

bus station

car park

playing fields

KEY

roads

pedestrian ways

teaching area

residential area

residential

communal facilities

group centres

restaurants

site boundaries

0 f   500 f   1000 f

York University, diagrams of science building development.

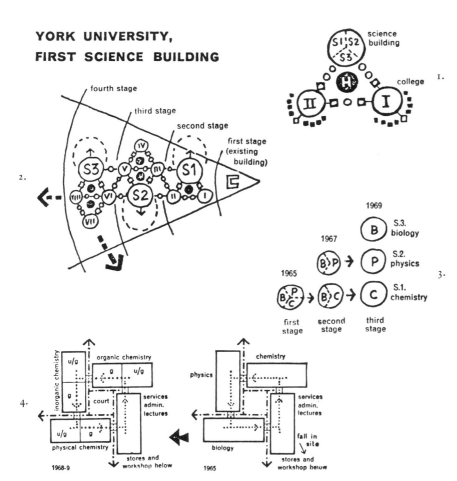

**YORK UNIVERSITY,
FIRST SCIENCE BUILDING**

1. Basic unit of university growth—the cell of the growing organism—
   a complex of two colleges with associated housing, and a science department,
   linked to each other by non-science departments; the whole enclosing one of
   the central buildings (e.g. concert hall, sports centre, library, etc.),
   whose unique function gives identity to the complex as a whole.
   The colleges also contain non-science teaching space.

2. Diagram of growth, relating the building program to stages of site
   development. One science department is built in each stage, and all three have
   room for expansion, without being isolated.

3. Stages of development of science buildings. Accommodation for physics,
   chemistry, and biology provided at all stages; each eventually
   has its own building.

4. Plan form of first science building, showing change from initial shared use
   by three departments to eventual sole use by one; and circulation routes
   planned to give insulation without isolation of graduate research from
   undergraduate teaching, and of the department from the rest of the community.

York University, diagrams of science building development.

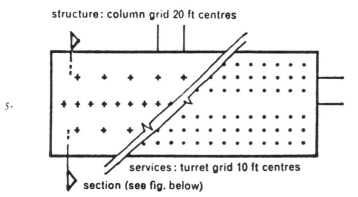

structure: column grid 20 ft centres

5.

services: turret grid 10 ft centres

section (see fig. below)

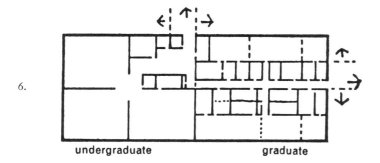

6.

undergraduate   graduate

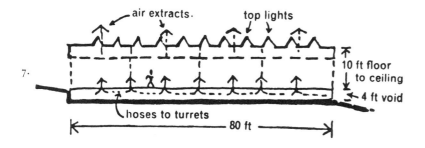

air extracts.   top lights

7.

10 ft floor to ceiling

4 ft void

hoses to turrets

80 ft

5. Plan showing internal column spacing and locations for removable service turrets.

6. Part plan, enlarged, showing partitioning (at stage three) and relation of graduate and undergraduate space. No partitions are structural.

7. Diagrammatic cross-section.

Utility turret designed for
York University. Architects: Robert Matthew,
Johnson-Marshall and Partners.

This kind of planning affords optimum flexibility, and requires no firm commitment to an architectural form. As a rational basis for planning it lends itself to decision-making on a democratic basis, a more difficult way to approach the process of planning than operating on intuition and group reflection, but in the long view more suitable for a university.

As an example of the present search for flexibility in teaching spaces, the York University science building is worth detailing.

The concept of a changing and dynamic university is basic to the total scheme, as shown in the diagrams on pages 30-31.

Several science departments are linked to a nonscience department to form a college. As the university expands, two of the science departments disengage to occupy their own quarters.

First-stage buildings are planned for gradual decanting: a 20-foot on-center column grid, specially designed turrets for services, and nonstructural partitioning admit easy change.

Each block can be divided into as many different laboratories, offices, and service areas as needed. Ten-foot ceiling heights are maintained throughout, lit from the top. A four-foot deep under-floor holds all water, gas, electric, and waste lines. Through flexible connections they are carried up to the appropriate fittings in movable turrets. The turrets can be turned 90 degrees.

By keeping all services in turrets, the laboratory benches can be no more than simple work tops. Mountable reagent trays and other devices can be added more cheaply than buying expensive, custom-built fixtures.

The mock-up of the turret shown to the left was constructed of sheet metal, painted with an epoxy-resin base and fully piped. Fittings are placed where needed, and unused outlets are blanked out. This is cheaper than providing a full range of fittings.

For organic chemistry the turret could take 10 water outlets, 4 vacuum pumps, 8 gas outlets, and 8 13-amp socket outlets. Extra services may be added: low voltage electricity, vacuum lines, and compressed air, though the trend is towards portable units at the bench for these services.

The four-foot underfloor space is also used as a plenum chamber for room temperature air under slight pressure. It is conducted up the turret and through the grilles at the top to be extracted through roof fans.

It would be wrong to imply that the architecture of teaching buildings has gone no further than turret design. England has a handful of admirable new buildings just completed. But here aesthetics are the overriding consideration rather than functional progress.

The engineering building at Leicester, for example, is an exciting building, one which is alternately praised and damned as being a likely candidate for widespread imitation.

Leicester breaks with the English traditions, with its unexpected juxtaposition of aluminium and red tile, towers and podium. The architects, Stirling and Gowan, have offered a valid alternative to the glass box and wall-punched facade.

The building's composition was arrived at on the basis of floor-loading, daylighting, and circulation requirements, plus a corner site that caused the units to be piled upwards.

Seen from the main approach, the complex is well marked by a 130-foot administrative tower, the top floor of which holds a water tank for the hydraulics laboratory on the ground level. On the east side is the small lecture hall, with four floors of research laboratories. Adjacent is the large lecture hall over which lie seven stories of offices and study rooms. Heavy loaded laboratories and

Nuffield Theatre, University of Southampton.
Sir Basil Spence, Bonnington and Collins, Architects.

special equipment areas are contained on the southwest side.

At Oxford the Physics Building by Ove Arup and Partners is similarly dramatic in its massing. The 100,000-square-feet, poured concrete building will include, among other items, a nuclear accelerator, an 800-seat lecture hall, and an apartment for the professor of physics. Along with the Nuffield Theatre at Southampton, these are good samples of recent designs, though it is the continuous teaching environment and the industrialized building which offer the most promise.

"It is a truism that a university is a society founded for the advancement of learning and the dissemination of knowledge. This means that it is constantly changing, always on its way, its work never completed. Departments expand, contract, quadruple in size, or virtually disappear within a few years, often in defiance of the most knowledgeable and expert forecasts.

Every building and each layout, so optimistically and thoroughly designed, seems to become within a decade not only out of date but physically hampering to the future. Any attempt therefore to constrict its movement artificially, either academically or physically, seems doomed, and rightly doomed, to failure."

CASSON AND CONDER
UNIVERSITY OF BIRMINGHAM DEVELOPMENT PLAN REPORT (1958).

THE CONTINUOUS TEACHING ENVIRONMENT

The continuous teaching environment resolves these dilemmas by taking a physical form that allows accreted growth and internal change, while encouraging maximum communication among the constituent parts of the institution.

At present it is Britain's major contribution to university development and has ready application to all levels of higher education in the United States.

This ideal differs from typical development patterns. It is not a centralized set of self-sufficient facilities scattered through a landscaped park or urban neighborhood; nor is it a series of secluded quadrangles casually linked to supporting buildings of a communal nature.

To be realized, obviously an abstraction of this kind must come to grips with realities such as site limitations, cost, staging, curriculum, and the minutiae of detailed assignments of space and equipment. In presenting the idea at Birmingham in 1958, Casson and Conder have identified some of the principles that suggest how it can work in an existing institution:

—Do not spread unnecessarily; a university should express itself as an entity by means of a compact and coherent layout.

—Keep open the access to possible long-term sites.

—Use the principle of the "joker"; allow undifferentiated space within areas set aside for specialized activities, this for sudden and previously unknown expansion.

—Use the principle of courtyard planning; completion of space by space; contrasting space to space.

—Discourage an architecture that imposes obligations. Except where there is obvious justification and certainty of the completion of the effect, design without dependence on symmetry and center-lines.

—Use the natural given personality of the site, demand that each building contribute to the special quality of the whole and not be something apart.

In furthering this idea at Birmingham, Casson and Conder are proposing the "street-deck" principle of expansion. They exploit the natural fall of the land by providing two buildings, one above the other, separated by an open pedestrian street deck.

The advantages of the scheme are these: high density without expensive lifts; a covered all-weather route linking all parts of the university; a strong architectural background to an area which is at the moment disorderly and without architectural coherence, and easy staging. The design can be threaded through existing buildings as illustrated on the next page. Access to parking and servicing is nicely solved.

As a form of comprehensive development, the scheme will be worth following, for it depends on a type of financial planning and academic programing unusual to present British procedures.

The main buildings would consist of a repetitive structural system that would accommodate a range of uses: study offices, laboratories, drawing offices, seminar rooms, and small lecture rooms. Large lecture rooms would be handled in specially designed auditoria connected to the street deck. Other specialized spaces not fitting into the basic grid could be attached in a similar fashion. Departments could be "tenants" for the space on a demand schedule using a computer calculated timetable. The architectural possibilities in this concept are well illustrated in the University of Leeds plan.

PRINCIPLE APPLIED DIAGRAM OF PRINCIPLE

CAR PARK

service

service

S.S   S.S   S.S

L.R.

POSSIBLE
FUTURE
EXTENSION

service

CIVIL ENGINEERING

COURTYARD

CHEMICAL ENGINEERING   COURTYARD

CAR PARK

UNIVERSITY ROAD WEST

BIOLOGY

CHEMISTRY

MECHANICAL
ENGINEERING

STREET DECK

old block   new block
CHEMICAL ENGINEERING

LONG ELEVATION

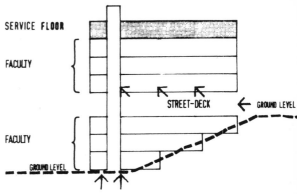

SERVICE FLOOR

FACULTY

STREET-DECK

GROUND LEVEL

FACULTY

GROUND LEVEL

REFECTORY

STAFF HOUSE

CHAMBERLAIN
TOWER

Street deck planning principle,
University of Birmingham.
Casson and Conder, Architects.

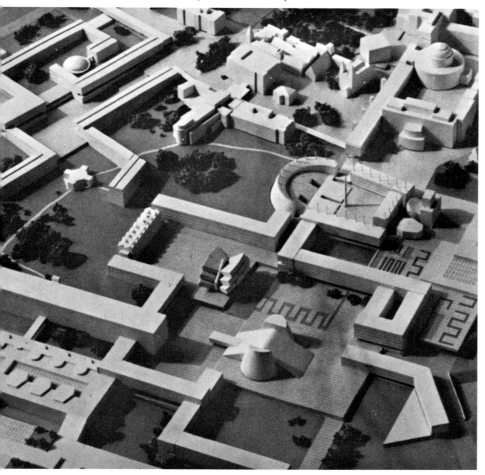

Model, central area, University of Leeds Development Plan.

UNIVERSITY OF LEEDS
DEVELOPMENT PLAN 1960/63
CHAMBERLIN, POWELL AND BON, ARCHITECTS

The Leeds planning effort is remarkable in two ways: the thoroughness of the programing and the forward-looking way in which the site was used to create the continuous teaching environment.

Leeds' existing buildings were spread in a crescent shape around the top of a hill, the center being a city reservoir and general cemetery. The campus was surrounded by an old and declining neighborhood, into which the University had casually placed some teaching buildings. Adjacent were four major hospitals used by the University Medical School. Redevelopment plans by the City called for extensive renewal nearby and the construction of a ring road which would have cut off the main campus from the town center and several of its teaching facilities.

Major design efforts in the new plan are focused on establishing a rational set of building types, the creation of as large a vehicular-free campus as possible, and the creative use of open spaces.

The new scheme exploits the proposed City ring road by placing it underground and reducing the number of through streets on the campus. The natural slopes are used for a connecting series of terraces and plazas which permit uninterrupted routes for people moving from the University to the town center or hospitals.

Building types are categorized by degree of flexibility. The rigid types, whose needs are known and not likely to change, are designed with great flair as special function buildings, and strung along the edges of the campus courts. These include the library, mathematics lecture halls (18 piled one on top of the other), physical education building, and administrative offices. They form the fixed core of the campus.

A second building type is those structures which have limited needs for internal change.

They are conceived as simple rectilinear, slablike blocks, four stories high and linked together.

The opposite extreme to the rigid buildings are those which have optimum flexibility for research: flexibility in form, servicing, and mechanical equipment. The requirements are met by using a modular series of dry wall structural components for production of light, disposable one-story enclosures. The spaces created, and their roofs and cladding would vary according to the program.

These research spaces are built on a concrete deck which is similar to the terraced pedestrian courts. The decks are raised sufficiently above ground to allow room for utilities to be fed up through the deck to the enclosed space above. The underground areas also contain the service roads to the buildings and parking space.

The siting of fixed and disposable structures is done so that the permanent multistory buildings define the new University core, while the flexible single-story units are allowed to spread out beyond the "facade" to the perimeter of the site.

The cemetery problem tested the ingenuity of the Leeds planners. "The problem," said Peter Chamberlin, "is that these valuable nine acres of open space occupied by the dead are also needed by the living. The prospect of having university buildings surround this open space is depressing but not because of it being a burial ground, but it is overcrowded, disarrayed, and badly neglected."

Accordingly the plan calls for renovating the plots into a living memorial. Some of the graves will be moved to new spots, the head-

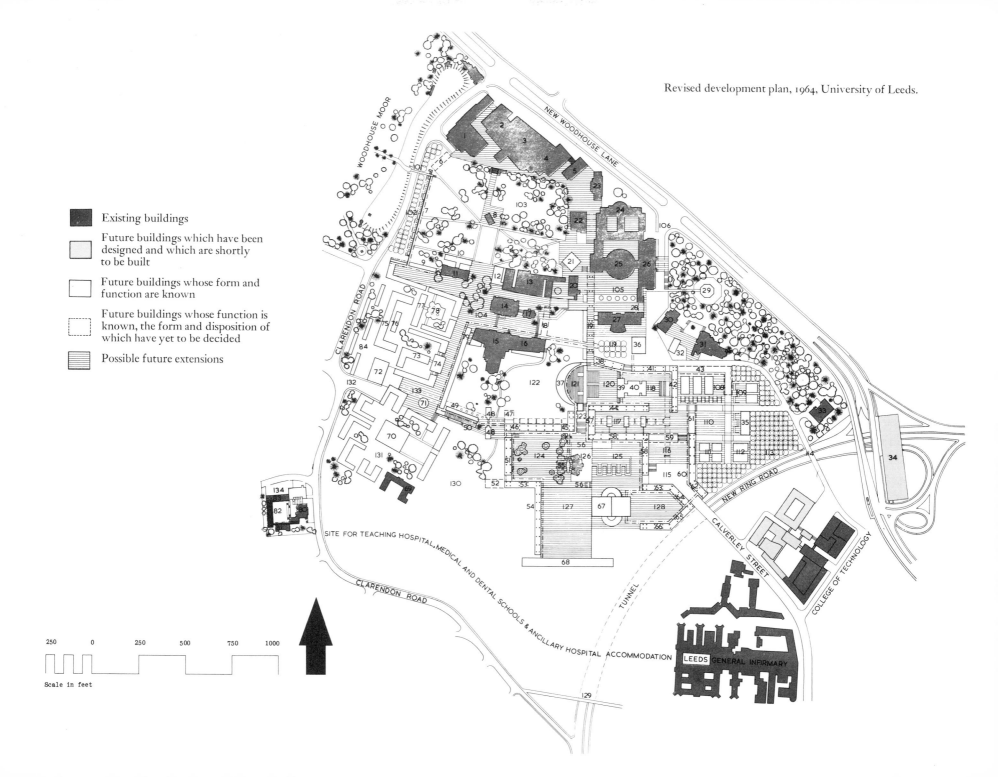

Revised development plan, 1964, University of Leeds.

Existing buildings

Future buildings which have been designed and which are shortly to be built

Future buildings whose form and function are known

Future buildings whose function is known, the form and disposition of which have yet to be decided

Possible future extensions

WOODHOUSE MOOR

NEW WOODHOUSE LANE

CLARENDON ROAD

NEW RING ROAD

CALVERLEY STREET

COLLEGE OF TECHNOLOGY

SITE FOR TEACHING HOSPITAL, MEDICAL AND DENTAL SCHOOLS & ANCILLARY HOSPITAL ACCOMMODATION

CLARENDON ROAD

TUNNEL

LEEDS GENERAL INFIRMARY

250   0   250   500   750   1000

Scale in feet

Three views, two in perspective and one in section, tell the story of the Mathematics Court, University of Leeds. Rendering, *upper left,* shows view of court looking toward the Senior Commons. *Lower left,* Mathematics-Geology building. Note high level bridges which link building to an electronic computer laboratory and lecture theatre. *Below,* cross-section, Mathematics-Geology building. Architects: Chamberlin, Powell and Bon.

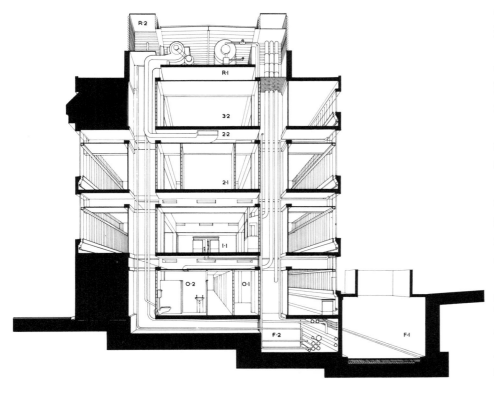

stones and monuments used as paved surfaces, grass and trees restored, and the walls pulled down so that the new garden-like quality might flow outwards to the University buildings.

The rational basis for building design, which is central to the concept of the continuous teaching environment, can be seen in the preliminary plans for the Mathematics-Geology building at Leeds.

The building is 50 feet wide, the maximum area that can be naturally lit by windows on opposite sides of the span with a 12-foot ceiling height.

Flexibility in service installations means that provision for both wet and dry utilities must be made. This in turn influences the spacing of supports and beam spans.

So that services may be installed later as needed, horizontal and vertical distribution conduits run the entire length of each floor between longitudinal and transverse structural beams, while vertical rising ducts are integrated with the columns.

As seen in the cross-section, left, a variety of functional spaces can be fitted into this modular planned building. The aesthetic effects are not diminished.

As an idea the continuous teaching environment can be extended to all aspects of university life, as the next pages will show. Seven new universities are being developed along these lines. Each differs from the others in important matters of educational policy and academic and social organization.

Their designs are equally divergent, both in broad form and in detail, but are still basically similar in the concept of continuity. This thrusting forward of a single idea, with many exciting variations, was probably not a conscious attempt, but in terms of the American scene it may well be Britain's most significant design concept for higher education.

UNIVERSITY OF ESSEX DEVELOPMENT PLAN 1963
ARCHITECT'S CO-PARTNERSHIP
C. K. CAPON, PARTNER-IN-CHARGE

Five of the first six new universities are located in cathedral towns and in parklike grounds. All are financed by UGC grants, supplemented by private fund drives. All start with full degree-giving powers and extensive differences in their educational philosophy. In this situation a Berkeley, California, -trained Vice-Chancellor and an internationally minded architect have combined to make Essex a bellwether in English university development.

They advance the idea that studies and curriculum cross administrative boundaries and that an interlocking, continuous teaching environment best expresses the future university. To avoid a split between teaching and social activities, housing is brought in close to the academic area, and facilities for leisure time pursuits are integrated with the academic buildings.

In complying with his brief the architect has placed the spine of the university in the valley of Wivenhoe Park. The main teaching buildings spread outwards and upwards over the slopes of the valley at right angles.

The central buildings bridge the valley, and all main services such as gas, heating, water, are carried underneath. The spine road gives access to the basements of the buildings. Car parks will be provided, as well as a bus station, thus separating vehicular from pedestrian traffic. The five consecutive, off-set platforms become intimate squares at the pedestrian level, and one is able to walk up the shallow steps from one platform to the next as on a raised street.

University of Essex, view of site looking towards playfields.
Opposite: Long-Range Development Plan.

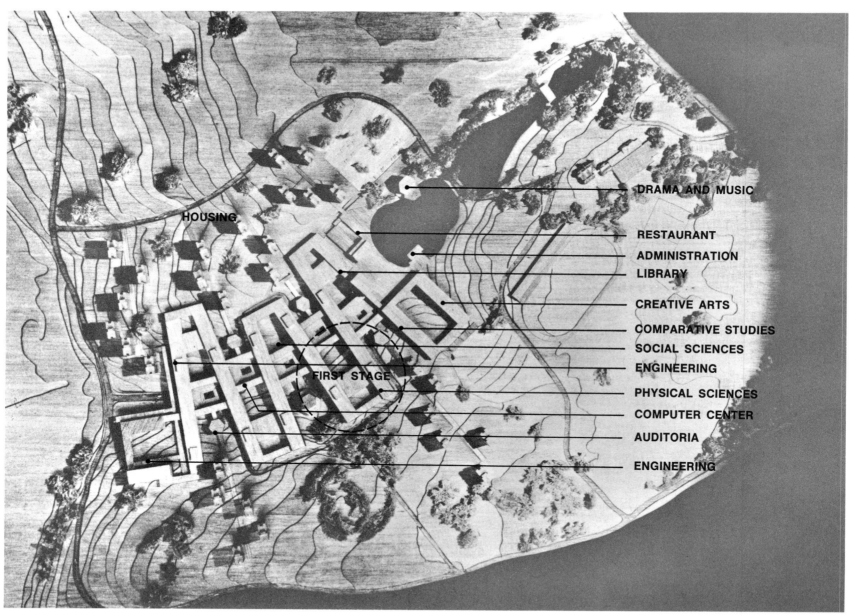

HOUSING

DRAMA AND MUSIC

RESTAURANT

ADMINISTRATION

LIBRARY

CREATIVE ARTS

COMPARATIVE STUDIES

SOCIAL SCIENCES

ENGINEERING

PHYSICAL SCIENCES

COMPUTER CENTER

AUDITORIA

ENGINEERING

FIRST STAGE

Long-Range Development Plan showing first stage.

Students will be accommodated in tower flats, which are snugly fitted between the riblike teaching buildings. For years to come, all students will be within three to five minutes walking distance of the university center.

Surplus earth from the foundation construction for the spine will help dam a third lake to the west of the built-up area, around which will be concentrated the intellectual and social life of the university: library, physical education center, administration building, and lakeside restaurant.

The economic advantages of compact development played a role in the final design. The valley allowed a relatively cheap way for segregating traffic and car parking. Essential services and roads do not have to be extended very far to reach every part of the site.

Concentration of teaching and research spaces meant that communal facilities such as reading rooms, coffee bars, squash courts, and service spaces get maximum use. In the long term, the total cost per square foot of usable space will be lower than with a dispersed development, and, in a country where land is scarce, sites should be used sparingly.

The 80 acres of built-up land will accommodate teaching, research, residential, and study facilities for 10,000 students. An additional 50 acres is reserved for playing fields, and the remaining 70 of the 200 acres is dedicated parkland.

Essex differs from York in that it is a continuous plan, with a density unprecedented in England. In the words of the Vice-Chancellor, A. E. Sloman, "It is a plan for a university town, not for some pavilions in the park.

"The architect's design, with buildings running into one another, reflects the wholeness of the university experience with no sharp division between work and leisure . . . as buildings are placed further from one another they have to become more self-sufficient; they need their own libraries and common rooms for example, and before you know what has happened they are isolated. Another serious danger is that in order to leave room for teaching and research buildings to expand, living accommodation gets pushed out to the edge of the site. You create a separate residential area, and unless you are careful the whole center of the university goes dead in the middle of the afternoon."

In addition to reflecting educational philosophy and economic constraints, Essex's design is equally concerned with the environmental needs of the people who will use the university during its growing pains. The pedestrian squares will help to shut out the noise and turmoil as the original nucleus is expanded.

There will, of course, always be some noise and movement at the main center. But the squares are purposively "designed large and the buildings around them all only three to four stories high so that sunshine can enter and the noise escape."

The new lake will open the center outwards to parkland. Students will be able to pass quickly, if they wish, from the crowded squares to quiet and privacy by the lakeside and in the park that surrounds it.

The essential features of the plan are thus:
—Conformity with the educational philosophy of maximum interdisciplinary contact.
—Integration of living and working areas.
—Separation of vehicular and pedestrian ways.
—A largely self-sufficient urban community.
—Optimum contrast between development and surrounding site.

University of Essex, view of first square.
Opposite: Floor plans show first teaching unit typical of design concept.

—A 24-hour university.

—Opportunity of limitless expansion.

The Vice-Chancellor aims to make a base for every university student. Fourteen-story towers, close to the academic center, will provide accommodation for both residents and nonresidents.

The top floor will house unmarried members of the academic staff, and the one below, married research students and graduates. The remaining 12 stories will be given over to undergraduates, separate floors for men and women.

Each floor will contain a 13-room flat, with service and kitchen facilities. The rooms will be furnished either as study-bedrooms for residents, or study rooms for those living off-campus. About one in three students will sleep in.

The idea is to encourage the students to use the university facilities intensively, and to avoid the artificial barriers that may be erected by dividing those who live on campus from those who must reside elsewhere.

Construction was begun with the pouring of the five platforms, shaping of the third lake, the laying of the initial spine road, and the foundation work for the tower building and a teaching block.

The latter is designed for the use of the physics building, but in the first years will accommodate several functions. It combines laser shock rooms with squash courts, lecture halls with faculty office, and meets the needs of a university in miniature.

Built of precast modular concrete, the teaching block will be connected on two levels to a large restaurant seating 500 students on two floors. On the balcony level there will also be a self-service snack bar and club rooms and on the lower level laundry facilities for students.

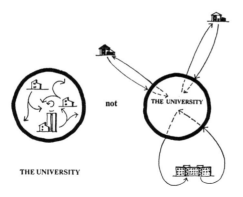

THE UNIVERSITY

The University—"a society of individuals living and working together for the advancement of learning and the dissemination of knowledge"

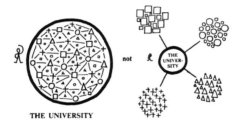

THE UNIVERSITY

The University—"a meeting place of different aptitudes, skills and specialisations"

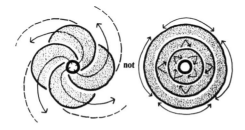

"Provision for easy growth and flexibility of use is vital"

UNIVERSITY OF YORK DEVELOPMENT PLAN 1962
ROBERT MATTHEW, JOHNSON-MARSHALL
AND PARTNERS
ANDREW DERBYSHIRE, PROJECT ARCHITECT

Many would date the beginning of contemporary university planning in Great Britain to the York report of 1963. If true, and it may be a moot point, the precedent for comprehensiveness belongs to Thomas Sharp and his work at Oxford, (1945) and Casson and Conder's plan for Birmingham, (1958); and for programmatic detailing, the Leeds scheme of 1960, Chamberlin, Powell and Bon.

Credits aside, the York scheme exemplifies the new spirit and significant emerging trends. Its merits begin with a Vice-Chancellor who wanted the best features of Oxbridge and the civic university style of education; and a group of architects challenged by his unusual academic brief.

York set out to establish a new relationship between teaching, library, social, and residential buildings. It argued for the natural association of students through their school of study, rather than through impersonal lecture halls or collegiate residential groupings.

The project architect, Andrew Derbyshire, has said that the communal nature of this type of academic organization had a direct bearing on the plan's physical form.

"The plan must be compact, have good internal communications to encourage contact between people, be capable of growth without disintegration, and provide for a clear hierarchy of identifiable and related groups from the individual to the whole so that each person and group can identify its own unique position in the university. Without this the university could never have sufficient cohesion to operate as a community but would remain merely a mass of isolated individuals."

As a new institution the form chosen for York was a cellular one, in which self-contained, teaching-residential buildings would slowly accrete into a full-scale university.

The fundamental cell is the college, genus York, whose size is the maximum number affording facial recognition after a year's regular contact. In number this means about 400 undergraduates, graduates, and academic staff; about half live in—including wives and children of the married residents.

Each college is assigned an association of related subjects called a department, and the departments make up the faculty. With the exception of science subjects which require laboratories, each department carries out its own building. (Special buildings are set aside nearby for the sciences. See page 50.)

The university teaching day was set at six hours in two periods: 9 a.m. to 1 p.m. and 5 p.m. to 7 p.m. This gave the students free time during the daylight hours on weekdays, and encouraged a large proportion of the university population living off the site to take advantage of the communal space provided for them in the college during the section breaks.

Four hundred people is an economic unit for a British dining hall and also allows each college to support leisure time and sports

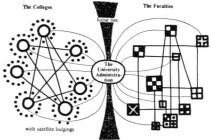

The Colleges   loose ties   The Faculties

The University Administration

with satellite lodgings

(a) OXFORD & CAMBRIDGE PATTERN

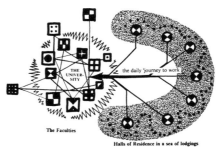

THE UNIVERSITY   the daily 'journey to work'

The Faculties

Halls of Residence in a sea of lodgings

(b) CIVIC UNIVERSITIES PATTERN

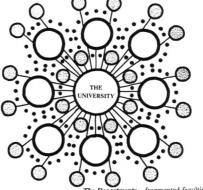

The Colleges with satellite housing and lodgings

THE UNIVERSITY

The Departments—fragmented faculties

(c) YORK PATTERN

University social and academic patterns compared.

49

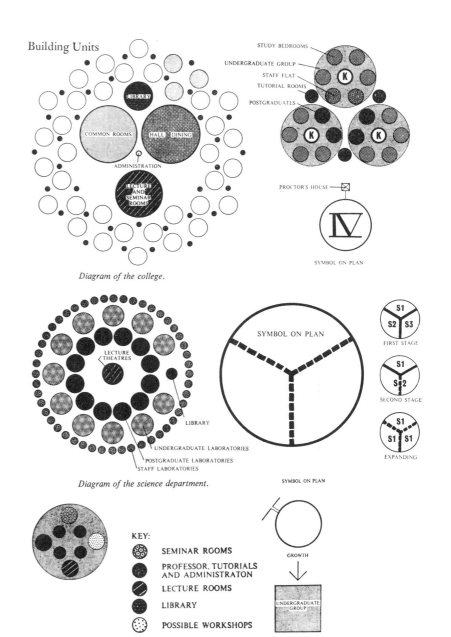

Building Units

STUDY BEDROOMS
UNDERGRADUATE GROUP
STAFF FLAT
TUTORIAL ROOMS
POSTGRADUATES

PROCTOR'S HOUSE

SYMBOL ON PLAN

Diagram of the college.

LECTURE THEATRES

LIBRARY

UNDERGRADUATE LABORATORIES
POSTGRADUATE LABORATORIES
STAFF LABORATORIES

SYMBOL ON PLAN

S1
S2 | S3
FIRST STAGE

S1
S2
SECOND STAGE

S1
S1 | S1
EXPANDING

Diagram of the science department.

SYMBOL ON PLAN

KEY:

- SEMINAR ROOMS
- PROFESSOR, TUTORIALS AND ADMINISTRATON
- LECTURE ROOMS
- LIBRARY
- POSSIBLE WORKSHOPS

GROWTH

UNDERGRADUATE GROUP

Diagram of the non-science department.

Relationships

The theoretical diagram applied to the site
and the building programme.

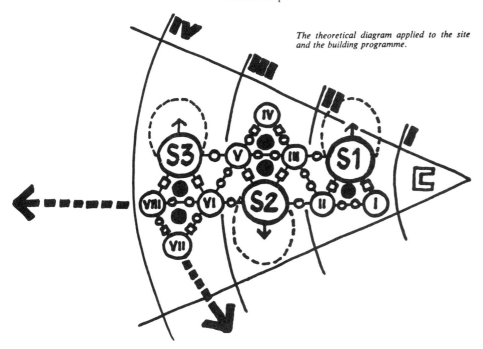

Plan concept (pages 50, 51): University of York development scheme.
Architects: Robert Matthew, Johnson-Marshall and Partners.

Colleges (numbered I to VIII with staff and student housing and some lecture and tutoria rooms)
— Main traffic routes
— Non-science department
— Science department
— Car parking areas
— Cycle and footways

0   500   1000 Feet

Heslington

clubs. But most importantly this size sustains at least three subject departments, thus avoiding academic as well as residential decentralization.

The eight colleges comprising the 3,200 student plan (10-year development) will be supported by a set of central facilities such as a sports center, concert hall, and central library. For the latter, each college will serve as an out-station for the main book collection, holding multiple copies of texts assigned to its department, as well as a selection of "light" reading and newspapers.

The University of York plan is notable for its conceptualization of the planning process. Diagrams from the report reproduced on page 49 show the basic organizational differences between the existing forms of British Universities and the York philosophy of education.

Other diagrams, opposite page, depict the primary residential unit, which consists of six study-bedrooms including room for an unmarried postgraduate student, tutorial room, and shared common space. Undergraduate groups are assembled into a college which also contains common rooms, library, college hall, and the college's share of lecture and seminar rooms. It is also possible to convert two undergraduate rooms into a graduate room. Head of college (provost) is accommodated in separate but nearby housing.

Nonscience units consist of lecture rooms, seminar rooms, etc. As noted, the science departments are housed in special laboratory buildings. Left: Basic diagram of university growth showing linkages between various units. The translation of the diagrams into architectural forms are shown on the next pages.

51

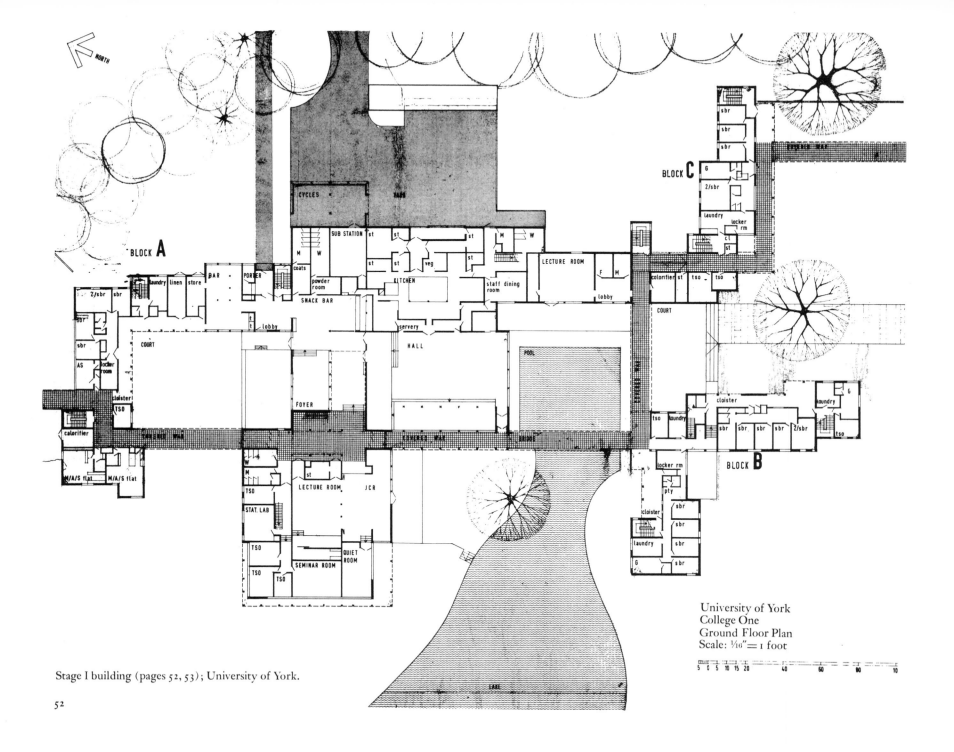

University of York
College One
Ground Floor Plan
Scale: 1/16" = 1 foot

5 0 5 10 15 20   40   60   80   10

Stage I building (pages 52, 53); University of York.

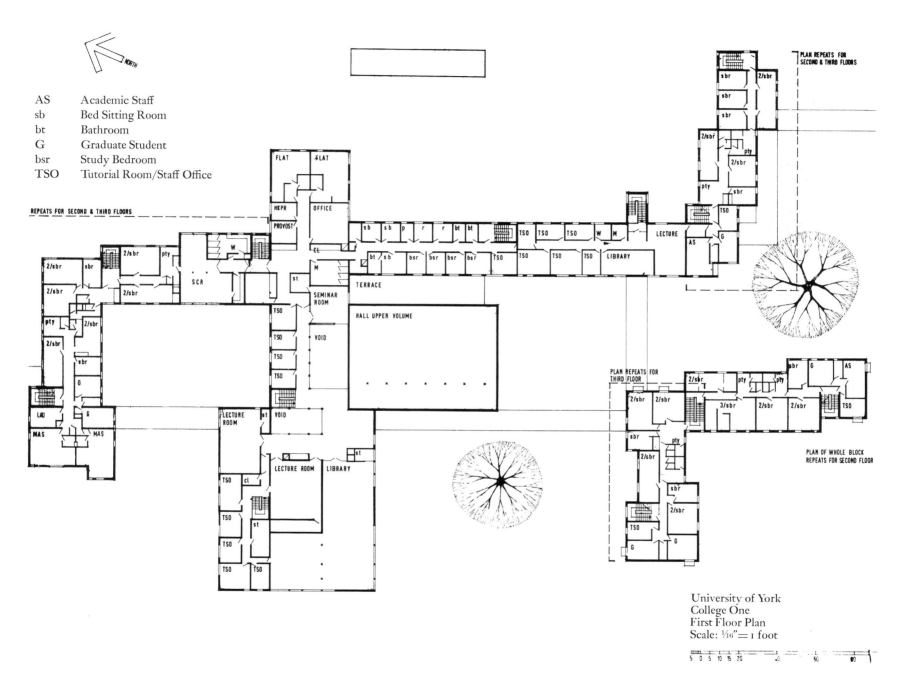

AS   Academic Staff
sb   Bed Sitting Room
bt   Bathroom
G   Graduate Student
bsr   Study Bedroom
TSO   Tutorial Room/Staff Office

NORTH

PLAN REPEATS FOR
SECOND & THIRD FLOORS

REPEATS FOR SECOND & THIRD FLOORS

PLAN REPEATS FOR
THIRD FLOOR

PLAN OF WHOLE BLOCK
REPEATS FOR SECOND FLOOR

University of York
College One
First Floor Plan
Scale: 1/16" = 1 foot

5 0 5 10 15 20   40   60   80

53

University of East Anglia, 6,000 student
development plan.
A—University Center
B—Teaching and research area
C—Residential areas

UNIVERSITY OF EAST ANGLIA
DEVELOPMENT PLAN 1963
DENYS LASDUN AND PARTNERS, ARCHITECTS

The land rises 70 feet from the river Yare facing a fine landscape. Site considerations and the academic brief underlie the design form.

Concentration was desired to "create a place where activities merge and where the individual can sense his identity with the whole," said Lasdun. "To derive full benefits the spread of the university must be limited; this also preserves the natural landscape."

The site allows road approach to the buildings at one or more floors above ground, giving a measure of concentration that could otherwise be obtained only by a more intensive use of elevators.

Building groupings fall into three functional categories, as seen in the model of the first draft scheme. The University center has a library for a million books and 2,000 reading places, an administrative block, assembly hall, small theater, university senate, and University House, the latter being the main dining hall and commons.

On the other side is a continuous belt of teaching and research facilities. This provides in any part of its length the various kinds of space required by a School of Study. The standardization which results makes it possible not only to use industrialized building methods in the structure but also an arrangement which allows future changes in internal layouts to be made.

The design embodies an academic principle of some importance. East Anglia will teach the full spectrum of university courses. Rather than place individual departments in separate buildings, cognate disciplines will be grouped into broadly based Schools of

Revised first stage plan.

Typical residential block.

Study. Arts and science teaching buildings have been intermingled to encourage contact by crossing of pedestrian ways, which are covered, all-weather passages.

Unlike the collegiate housing at York, a mixed residential grouping was considered unimportant, though half of the long range enrollment (3,000 students) will be housed on campus in accommodations directly connected to the teaching areas.

Residential blocks are constituted around social units of 12 people or less. Each group will have its own entrances, kitchen, breakfast room, and bathrooms. Groups of rooms can be set aside for men or women undergraduates, or combined into flats for single or married tutors or undergraduates.

Residential blocks will be stepped up the hill to create an undercroft on the north side overlooking the river. Units will be linked to the teaching areas by stairs and high-level decks. Garages, stores, games rooms, squash courts, and workshops will be located below.

First stage development will include about one-half of the eventual (1) Library, (2) University House, (3) Arts, (4) Chemistry, and (5) Biology buildings and (6) 10 residential blocks. (See model photograph, this page.)

As an interim measure awaiting construction of the permanent buildings, the university has opened a "temporary" university for the first 800 students on an adjacent site.

Erected in the remarkably short period of nine months, using prefabricated materials, the "academic village" contains 88,000 square feet of various teaching facilities, plus common rooms and assembly hall. This made it possible for the university to undertake both teaching and research in the sciences in its foundation year.

The site was planned generally for single-story units with the exception of the arts accommodations. Small ancillary elements such as boiler house, telephone exchange, and lavatories were built in brick, the remainder in light timbered panel construction. To reduce the chances of fire spreading, 30 feet was allowed between buildings, and a rough track surrounds all to allow easy access for emergency vehicles to all buildings.

This fortuitous event will now enable the university to step up its scheduled enrollments, and given the pressure of increasing numbers it is likely that the village will be fully occupied for some time ahead.

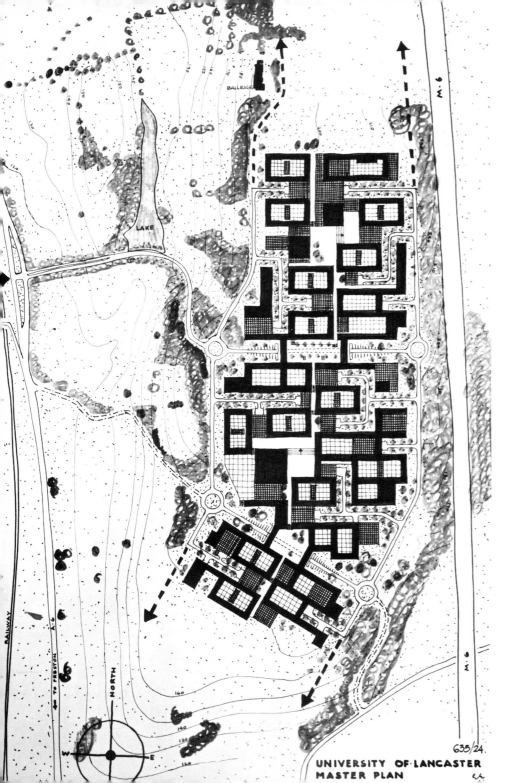

UNIVERSITY OF LANCASTER
DEVELOPMENT PLAN 1964, ACCOMMODATIONS
FOR 7,000 NONRESIDENTIAL STUDENTS
DESIGNED BY
BRIDGEWATER, SHEPHEARD & EPSTEIN

An essential feature of the Lancaster plan is a long, flexible campus spine, running north and south as a continuous colonnaded pedestrian walkway, opening here and there into squares which are formed by the university colleges. Each college is a basic study-social-teaching unit. The public facilities such as coffee bars, shops, dining rooms, commons, face the spine. Interspersed among the colleges are University-wide facilities: libraries, religious center, assembly halls. These too are arranged around squares and plazas.

"We see the colleges as being part of a continuous, lively high street, rather than a secluded campus," commented the Vice-Chancellor. He added, "We want students here at night, this is not to be a nine-to-five university."

The site is bounded by a railway and major regional highways. The building zone is placed on high and relatively level land on the east side of the site. To the west the land slopes steeply away with magnificent views to the sea. A long screen of woodland happily cuts off noise from the major motorway.

The main approach road comes from the west, past an existing but enlarged lake, and up and through the existing woods. It connects to a ring road that surrounds the built-up area. This in turn is

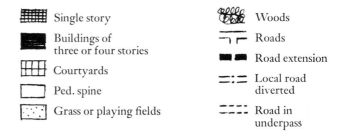

▦ Single story		⟨⟨⟨ Woods	
◼ Buildings of three or four stories		⊤⊤ Roads	
▦ Courtyards		■ ■ Road extension	
▢ Ped. spine		⹀⹀ Local road diverted	
▢ Grass or playing fields		- - - Road in underpass	

University of Lancaster: Central Square

joined by a tunnel under the main square, where the campus bus station will be located: at this central interchange point passengers leave the bus and emerge upstairs.

Most of the students will live off-campus, under present assumptions. Parking will be provided in landscaped cul-de-sacs tucked behind the various college buildings. This reduces the need for large lots and long walking distances from cars to buildings.

As shown in the drawing to the left, if the university expands further, underpasses would be located every quarter of a mile in order to connect the two sides of the ring road.

The university is planned on a grid system that runs about 135 feet north and south. Most buildings are 35 feet deep, and the spaces between form squares about 100 feet wide. Some of the interior study lounges are to be designed for possible conversion into residential units at a later date.

All structures are to be of precast concrete with three and four stories as maximum height for economy of construction and cheapest circulation—*au pied*. The length of the spine which connects the building groups has been set at a quarter of a mile per 3,500 stu-

dents, and all services run under. Drainage falls outwards and down to main drains along the periphery roads.

Since the University advocates a mixing of various department buildings, expansion is handled by adding squares as needed and lengthening the spine north and south. Additional expansion for colleges fixed in place can be handled east and west away from the initial construction.

The designers intend in this way to ensure an undisturbed environment by keeping new construction to the edges of the campus.

What might in other hands be a static and dull functional solution is enlivened in several ways: the repeating squares are staggered down the spine, design treatment in each open space will differ in details, rooflines vary in accordance with the functions of the building, and the activities along the spine animate the total scheme.

The siting of the continuous buildings protects pedestrians from the prevailing west winds. The squares are oriented mostly east and west for maximum sunlight. By spreading out the activity points, the University carries on an old British tradition: getting from place to place will be half the fun.

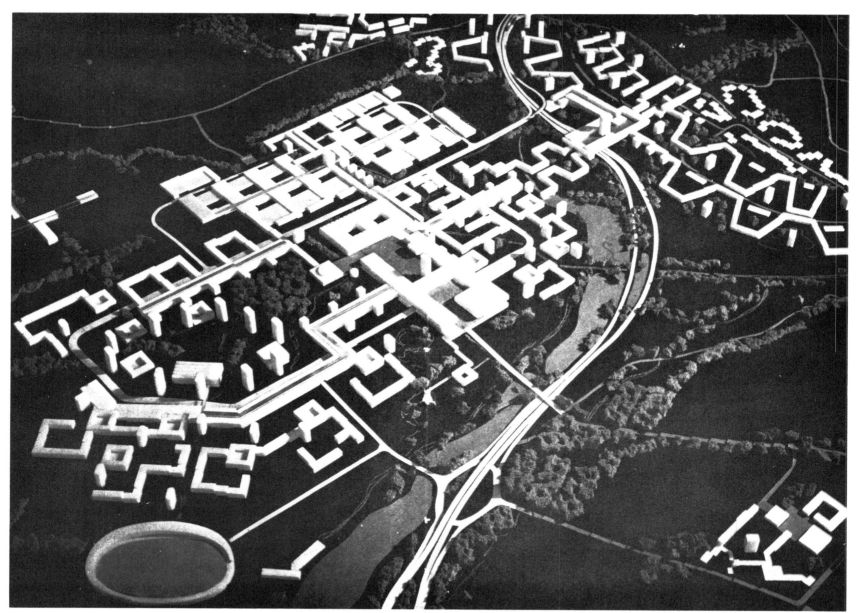

University of Warwick, model of plan at 15,000 student level. *Right:* Campus center.

UNIVERSITY OF WARWICK
LONG-RANGE DEVELOPMENT PLAN 1964
DESIGNED BY LING AND GOODMAN

Warwick stands out in size from all other new British universities. The plan accommodates 15,000 students, two-thirds in residence. Capital construction costs are estimated at $162 million.

Basically the scheme attempts to create a tight, compact urban campus, in contradistinction with the Green Belt in which it is situated. Residential halls are interwoven into the academic areas so as to be effectively used for feeding, working, and social activities throughout the day. No physical recognition is given to individual schools or departments. Instead a university-wide atmosphere is favored, though the humanity areas are separate and distinct from the science areas because of the building types involved.

Fundamental to the design was the concept of encouraging all members of the University to see themselves as belonging to a single society, and at the same time being able to develop personal allegiance to a group smaller than the university as a whole.

The Halls were designed to provide a social and work space for 1,000 students each, a third of whom would be living off-campus. The Halls would be located to serve as a link between the teaching areas and the residential accommodations.

"Those belonging to the Hall will comprise a mixture of academic disciplines, of men and women, of younger and older students, and of residents and nonresidents.

"Accommodations will vary from study-bedrooms for those fresh from school to flatlets for graduate students. The nonresident student in particular will use the Hall as his effective base in the uni-

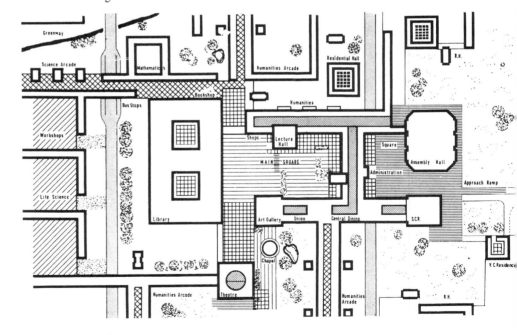

Central Area Diagram

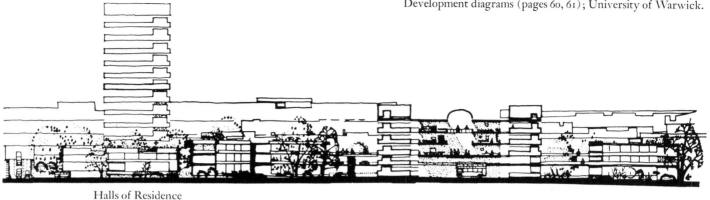

Halls of Residence

Diagrammatic section showing principle of an arcade adjoining a hall of residence.

versity. He will eat in the Hall refectory, use the Hall car park and laundry, and have a personal locker, and will gain by this means a greater sense of belonging to the University."

As in several other university schemes the campus is separated from the nearby regional highways by limited access roads, and, inside the campus, vehicles and pedestrians are segregated by using changes of topography to bridge over the internal service loop roads. Bus service is provided inside the campus. Pedestrians will move along arcaded walkways which run through the major buildings. Walks and roads join at the University Center.

The Center is a paved court around which are situated the Assembly Hall, Theater, Administrative offices, Chapel, Library, Union building and shops. Car park and bus depot are under the main square.

From the Center the teaching arms stretch out in three directions in the form of arcaded pedestrian streets. The arm to the west leads to the science area, the others into the humanities buildings. The plan allows for lateral, longitudinal, and vertical growth, with the center to be completed as early as possible, later expansion will occur outwards.

The built-up areas are surrounded by playfields which help to maintain the Green Belt in which the university is situated as well as to give contrast to the campus form. Water sports (boating and swimming) will take place in the lake running north and south along the edge of the campus. Nearby is the major university stadium, sited within 2,000 feet of the campus center.

To the west the architects have included in the scheme a university-related neighborhood of 7,000 people. A shopping center and a hotel are constructed on air rights, over the highway, in the form of a plaza which links university and neighborhood.

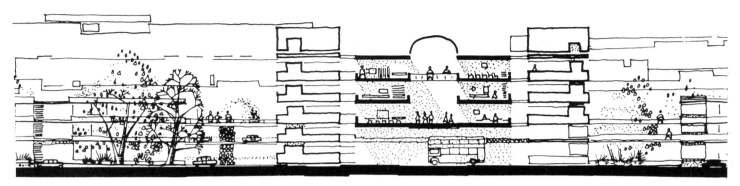

Diagrammatic section showing the principles of an arcade.

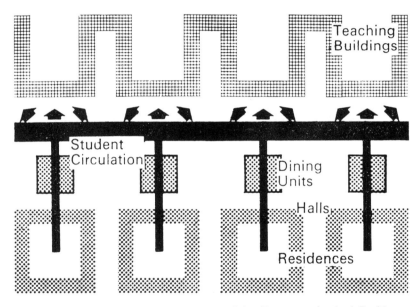

Teaching Buildings

Student Circulation

Dining Units

Halls

Residences

Dining Rooms serving both Residences
and Teaching Buildings

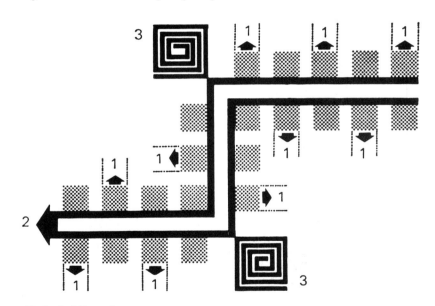

3

2

Method of Growth
1. Expansion of Existing
   Subjects from their initial
   position.
2. Expansion of Further Subjects.
3. New Growth Points.

UNIVERSITY OF SURREY DEVELOPMENT PLAN 1964
BUILDING DESIGN PARTNERSHIP

The University of Surrey was founded in 1894 as Battersea Polytechnic Institute and is one of the first Colleges of Advanced Technology to advance to university status as recommended by the Robbins report. Existing buildings are to be abandoned.

Though Guildford's population is less than 60,000 people, the town was selected for the new location because the community serves as a shopping and cultural center for an area containing over three-quarters of a million people within a 15-mile radius. Important national research establishments are maintained nearby at Farnborough, Leatherhead, Bracknel, and Teddington. The University will vigorously promote research in similar fields. About two-thirds of the anticipated enrollments will be in the sciences and engineering.

Faced with the choice of two sites, the planners of the University of Surrey have wisely opted to use both.

The circulation system will connect the central campus to the town center less than a mile away. To the west, a similar link will be maintained to an adjacent 290-acre playfield and expansion area.

Seen from the distance, the initial 80-acre development for 5,000 students will appear as a compact hill town surrounding the Guildford Cathedral.

Plan, University of Surrey.

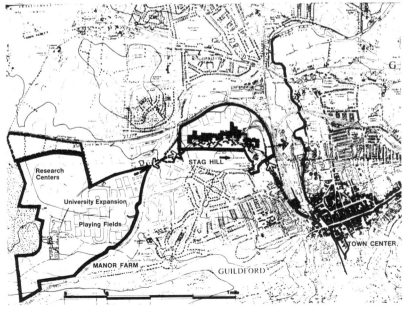

Three building zones—residential, social, and academic—follow the contours below the crest of the hill in compact linear form.

Residential facilities are informally sited in 3- to 12-story buildings in the band nearest the Cathedral. The structures are designed to provide kitchen, breakfast room, laundry, and service space for groups of 12 students. Each group of 12 can be combined vertically or horizontally to form "houses" of 50 students or less; and the houses in turn can be expressed architecturally as a social group of 500 or less students.

The northern band contains the teaching buildings, with departmental and administrative office space and research laboratories. In contrast with the continuous band of residential towers, these are "a broken wall" through which there will be glimpses of the various buildings on the hill.

In the central band the communal buildings—dining halls, kitchens, club rooms, library, senate, and others—serve as a link between the residences and the academic area and are connected to both by a series of staircases, high level pedestrian streets, and lift shafts.

The university is planned as a self-contained enclave. Segregation of pedestrians from vehicles is a major feature of the scheme. Through traffic is kept to the boundaries. Service roads from the east and west come together under the communal areas. Provision is made there for parking 320 staff cars. Student parking for about 3,000 cars is to be handled in large lots at the northern end of the university precinct, and separated by playing fields.

The schedule expenditures call for construction in the order of $4.2 million annually for three years, with accommodation for 3,000 students at the end of the period. To achieve the targets, industrialized building components will be utilized with a high proportion of prefabricated components.

The social buildings and residential facilities are expected to remain constant in their form and use, with expansion handled by linear growth towards the 290 acres adjacent, while academic buildings are most likely to be the focus of substantial growth and change.

However, in place of accommodations tailor-made to the specific requirements of each department, which could lead to rapid obsolescence, Grenfell Baines and his architects have come up with a new form of universal space.

Essentially it is an "L" shaped building, stepped in section. The top floor provides rooms for staff and administrative offices and small seminar spaces. The middle floors can accommodate classrooms and laboratories. Workshops, heavy machinery, and large laboratories are taken care of on the ground floor.

The basic "L" shape can be extended to form a "U." Two "U's" can combine to form an "O" and the closed "O's" can form independent chains for expansion to the north.

In the designer's eye, Surrey will evoke the image of a craggy hill town leading to the steps of Guildford Cathedral.

UNIVERSITY OF SUSSEX STAGE I
DEVELOPMENT PLAN 1960
SIR BASIL SPENCE, BONNINGTON
& COLLINS, ARCHITECTS

Sussex appropriately ends this review of new British University development. Unlike the other schemes, the first stage construction is finished and the beauty of site and architecture reminds us that the campus is also an art form.

Designed by the architects of Coventry Cathedral, Sussex was meant from the beginning to be a statement of aesthetic unity. The structures are among the most handsome in postwar England, free from the potpourri of cladding that mars so many other buildings.

The tall beeches and rolling downs set the scale for the buildings, none of which is higher than three stories. On the exterior only three materials are in evidence, all indigenous to the county: a warm red brick, board-marked concrete, and knapped flint panels. Through the use of arcades and vaults, a continuity in design is maintained, though massing and detailing of buildings change with function.

The site, leased for 999 years from the estate of the Earl of Chichester, was chosen in part because the University could make arrangements to house two-thirds of its students at off-season rates in resort hotels and boarding houses in nearby Brighton.

Sussex is small compared to the other new universities: 1,500 students in the first stage, 3,000 students in the long-range plan. Initial construction was centered around Falmer House (dining rooms, commons, and recreation rooms) and reflects the University's desire to create a corporate life and the university tradition as early as possible. Buildings for chemistry, physics, the arts, and a library com-

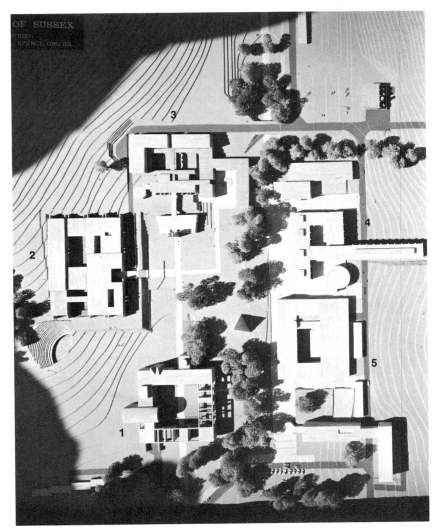

Model, phase one construction.
1. Falmer House
2. Library
3. Arts complex
4. Chemistry
5. Physics and Mathematics
Opposite: Falmer House .

plete the first stage development. The latter will accommodate 280,-000 volumes and 700 readers. The initial buildings are grouped around a major quadrangle. All are well planned, comfortable, neither experimental nor old-fashioned—they "simply work well."

Sussex has been coolly received by the British architectural press and considered by many observers to be the last of its kind. The purists complain that the structural system is masked for aesthetic effect rather than function—and it is; the cast concrete vaults are thin shells hung from the concrete ribs and are not structure-giving elements. Costs averaged around 140 shillings per square foot for the first two buildings, in comparison with 80 shillings for a typical CLASP building. Yet the aesthetic effects cannot be denied, and, accordingly, Sussex has gained a pride of place that gives a special

dimension to their vigorous academic program.

Sussex thus exemplifies the British dilemma. The new university designs are meeting the challenges of time, money, and an overburdened building industry. The idea of a continuous environment for learning has emerged: an environment capable of expansion and change, having suitable variety in architectural form and content, and reflecting a pattern of site development that is concerned about group as well as individual values in a fast growing society.

To succeed however, art must match technology in the detailing of the new schemes. The dreary and the dull, by-products of expediency, must be overcome and, if they can, then the ideas present in the new universities will have long-lasting consequence not just for the American scene, but for Britain itself.

Far left: Falmer House: Voids on upper floors form roof terraces; will be filled later as expansion
space is required, with minimum structural work and disruption of activities within building.
Left: Library building. *Above:* View from Falmer House courtyard. Library to the left, arts building straight on.

CREDITS

ACKNOWLEDGEMENTS

We acknowledge with thanks the help of the following
in obtaining plans and drawings reproduced in this report.

William Allen

O. Grenfell Baines

Michael Brawne

Michael Brooks

C. K. Capon

Peter Chamberlin

Gordon Collins

Neville Conder

A. Cranshaw

Andrew Derbyshire

Terry Devlin

Claire Brake Dober

Gabriel Epstein

Brian Falk

L. H. Fauber

R. H. Float

P. D. B. Groves

Michael Kendall

Denys Lasdun

A. D. Linfoot

Leonard Manasseh

Peter McKenley

Hugh Morris

Alexander Redhouse

Richard Sheppard

Ronald H. Sims

A. E. Sloman

Robert Smart

A. V. Smith

W. L. Waide

J. Whittam

Richard P. Dober is a principal in the firm of Dober, Walquist and Harris, Inc., Cambridge, Massachusetts. He has served as Visiting Critic and Lecturer in the Graduate School of Design, Harvard University and is a frequent contributor to professional journals. Recent professional assignments include programing studies for Massachusetts Institute of Technology, a long range plan for the University of Guelph, Guelph, Ontario, and development studies for the Central American Management Institute. Mr. Dober is the author of "Campus Planning," published by the Reinhold Publishing Corporation in 1964 and has served as an EFL consultant on college planning.